Martin Luther King Jr.

Marching for Equality

Stephanie E. Macceca

Consultant

Glenn Manns, M.A.
Teaching American History Coordinator
Ohio Valley Educational Cooperative

Publishing Credits

Dona Herweck Rice, *Editor-in-Chief*; Lee Aucoin, *Creative Director*; Conni Medina, M.A.Ed., *Editorial Director*; Jamey Acosta, *Associate Editor*; Neri Garcia, *Senior Designer*; Stephanie Reid, *Photo Researcher*; Rachelle Cracchiolo, M.A.Ed., *Publisher*

Image Credits

cover Library of Congress; p.1 Library of Congress; p.4 Ullstein Bild/The Granger Collection; p.5 Library or Congress, LC-USZ62-122985; p.6 (left) Library of Congress, LOC_057135pu, (right) jimbowen0306/Flickr; p.7 Khlobystov Alexey/Shutterstock; p.8 (top) Library of Congress, LC-USZ62-134433, (bottom) Eileen Meyer/Shutterstock; p.9 Keith R. Neely; p.10 Library of Congress, LC-USF33-T01-001112-M1; p.11 Library of Congress, LC-USF33-020522-M2; p.12 National Museum of American History, Smithsonian Institution; p.13 Library of Congress, LC-USZ62-126559; p.14 Michael Ochs Archives/Getty Images; p.15 (top) Donald Uhrbrock/Getty Images, (bottom) New York Times/Getty Images; p.16 The Granger Collection; p.17 Don Cravens/Getty Images; p.18 Library of Congress, LC-USZ62-125957; p.19 (top) Wikimedia; (bottom) Rue des Archives/The Granger Collection; p.20 Donald Uhrbrock/Getty Images; p.21 Library of Congress, LC-DIG-ppmsca-08129; p.22 Rue des Archives/The Granger Collection; p.23 (top) Associated Press, (bottom) Popperfoto/Getty Images; p.24 JustASC/Shutterstock; p.25 Associated Press; p.26 DoD/Newscom; p.27 AFP/Getty Images; p.28 (left) Don Cravens/Getty Images, (right) Time & Life Pictures/Getty Image; p.29 (left) Rue des Archives/The Granger Collection, (right) AFP/Getty Images; p.32 (top left) Rock the Vote, (bottom left) Visions of America, LLC / Alamy, (right) Lisa F. Young/Shutterstock

Teacher Created Materials
5301 Oceanus Drive
Huntington Beach, CA 92649-1030
http://www.tcmpub.com

ISBN 978-1-4333-1589-3

Printed in China
Nordica.012019.CA21801586

Table of Contents

Introduction

Martin Luther King Jr. changed America. At the time, laws made life hard for **African Americans** in the South. He spoke out about these unfair laws. He said all people should be treated the same. He gave speeches and led marches to tell the world about the problem.

Fun Fact

Martin also spoke out against poverty and war.

People protesting the war

Martin giving a speech

Martin's Childhood

Martin was born on January 15, 1929. He lived in Atlanta, Georgia, with his parents and his grandparents. He had an older sister and a younger brother. His mother taught them how to play the piano. She was a teacher. His father was a **minister**.

Martin's childhood church and home

Fun Fact

Martin's real name was Michael. His father changed his name to Martin after a family trip to Europe. Martin was only five years old.

Martin's route from Atlanta, Georgia, to Europe

Martin attended a school like this when he was a young boy.

Fun Fact

Martin wanted to be a firefighter when he grew up.

As a boy, Martin liked to play football and baseball. He had a paper route. His best friend was white. When the boys started school, Martin was not allowed to play with his white friend any more.

Martin on his paper route

When Martin was young, African American children could not go to school with white children. They could not go to the same restaurants (RES-ter-ahnts). They could not use the same bathrooms. They could not drink from the same drinking fountains. African Americans had to sit in the back seats of city buses.

A young African American boy taking a drink of water

The laws that separated African Americans from whites in public places were called **Jim Crow Laws**.

An African American waiting for the bus

Martin was a bright student. He finished high school at age 15. He went to Morehouse College like his father and his grandfather. He studied to be a minister. He continued his studies. In 1955, he earned a **doctorate** (DOK-ter-it) **degree**.

Martin on graduation day

Fun Fact

Martin skipped both the ninth and twelfth grades of high school.

Helping Others

Martin became a minister in Montgomery, Alabama. He was famous for his great speeches. He spoke out about laws that were unfair to African Americans. He wanted to change the laws. He became a **civil rights** leader. Rights are things that make life fair for everyone.

Martin giving a speech

Martin speaking at a church

Fun Fact

Martin first thought he might be a lawyer or a doctor.

Rosa sitting at the front of a public bus

One day in 1955, Rosa Parks sat in the front of a Montgomery city bus. It was against the law for African Americans to sit in the front. But Rosa would not move to the back of the bus. The police took her to jail. Martin said this was wrong. He asked all African Americans to **boycott** (BOI-kot), or stop riding, city buses.

Thousands of people boycotted buses. This cost the bus company a lot of money.

The boycott lasted more than a year. Finally, the city agreed to let African Americans sit anywhere they wanted. Martin's plan had worked. But more laws needed to be changed. Some people wanted to fight for change. But Martin would only use **nonviolent** ways.

African Americans and a white man sitting together on a bus

Fun Fact

Martin met Mohandas Ghandi (GAHN-dee) in India. Ghandi also believed in nonviolence.

People marching in support of Martin

Martin gets arrested after a protest

Marching On

Between 1957 and 1968, Martin traveled around the United States. He helped African Americans sign up to vote. He gave speeches and led marches against unfair laws. He led a huge protest in Birmingham, Alabama. He went to jail many times for his work.

Martin traveled over six million miles. He gave more than 2,500 speeches.

In 1963, Martin led a march in Washington, D.C. More than 250,000 people came. On the steps of the Lincoln Memorial, Martin gave his most famous speech. He spoke about his dreams for America. His said he wanted all Americans to share equal freedoms.

Martin giving his famous "I Have a Dream" speech

Fun Fact

This march led to the Civil Rights Act, which made equality the law.

President Johnson signing the Civil Rights Act

Martin's Dream

Martin's ideas made some people mad. Many Southerners wanted African Americans and whites to stay separate. They did not want the laws to change. One of these angry men shot Martin on April 4, 1968. Martin died at the age of 39.

A newspaper from the day Martin was killed

Martin's family at his funeral

The world remembers Martin Luther King Jr. as a hero. Every January, America celebrates his birthday. Martin had a dream that one day all people would be treated the same. He gave his life to make this dream come true.

President Ronald Reagan signed a law to make Martin Luther King Jr. Day a federal holiday.

Fun Fact

Martin Luther King Jr. won the Nobel (noh-BEL) Peace Prize. He was the youngest winner ever.

Time

1929
Martin Luther King Jr. is born in Atlanta, Georgia.

1955
The bus boycott begins in Montgomery, Alabama.

1963
Martin gets arrested.

Line

1963
Martin gives his "I Have a Dream" speech in Washington, D.C.

1964
The Civil Rights Act is signed.

1964
Martin wins the Nobel Peace Prize.

1968
Martin is killed on April 4, at the age of 39.

Glossary

African Americans—Americans whose families first came from Africa

boycott—to not buy from or give business to

civil rights—the rights that every citizen has

doctorate degree—the highest type of college degree

equality—a situation in which people from different groups have the same rights

Jim Crow Laws—laws that kept African Americans unequal to white people

minister—a religious leader

nonviolent—peaceful

protest—action or words that show disagreement with something

Index

Americans Today

Rock the Vote is a group of people who care about civil rights. The people in the group believe that everyone should be treated the same. The goal of the group is to educate young people and encourage them to vote.